The Magic Ear

Orca Book Publishers

The Magic Ear

Story by Laura Langston

Illustrations by Victor Bosson

n a small island in Northern Japan lived a poor but honest young peasant named Hoderi. He was a kind and happy man, though he laboured many long hours in the garden of the local nobleman.

Every morning when the tide was low, Hoderi hurried along the beach from his simple hut to the luxurious estate of his employer. As he walked, he loved to watch the waves of the sea crest and dip and crest some more. And he always took time to observe the tiny sea creatures playing in the shallow tidepools.

One morning Hoderi noticed a baby sea bream chased into a small tidepool by a large, angry fish. Hoderi quickly clapped his hands together — one, two, three — and the large fish swam away. The little sea bream, however, flapped helplessly about in the shallows.

"You must leave that place," Hoderi told the tiny fish. "There is not enough water for you." He reached down, and with the kindness that was in his nature, carefully placed the little fish in deeper water. "Swim away as fast as you can, where that big fish will not find you."

Hoderi turned to go, happy that he had done a good deed, and so early in the morning. But he had not gone many more steps before he heard a voice behind him calling, "Hello. Hello. Please wait."

Behind him was a woman with a face so beautiful and clothes so exquisite he was sure she must be a goddess. Knowing he had never seen a woman so lovely before, and knowing she would want nothing with him, a poor peasant, he turned away.

The woman called again. "You there! Please wait! I am a messenger from the king of Neriya. You have saved the life of his only daughter, and I have come to take you beneath the waves to his kingdom in the sea."

"I cannot go," Hoderi said in his true and honest way, "for I am unable to swim."

The woman smiled. "You do not need to swim," she said. "Come to the edge of the water with me. I am really a fish, and I will take you safely to the kingdom of Neriya."

And so Hoderi walked to the edge of the sea, where the woman turned into a huge carp. Without another word, he climbed onto her back, and together they began their descent beneath the waves.

oderi entered the dragon king's palace as the much-awaited guest. All the subjects of Neriya stood before him. The dragon king himself bowed low in his honour. At the king's side stood his daughter, who was transformed into a woman even more beautiful than the messenger who had first stopped him on the beach. She had long black hair that fanned through the water like clouds of silk. Her flowing robe glistened like the underside of a wave. And when she spoke, her voice sounded like music on the water.

"Thank you for saving my life," the daughter said. "I never would have escaped from that fish if you had not helped. And if I had escaped, I surely would have drowned in that shallow pond."

Hoderi lowered his head before such majesty. "It was nothing," he answered in his true and honest way. "I would have done it for anyone. I would do it again."

And so the great feasting began. Finally, after much dancing and rejoicing, the great dragon king turned to Hoderi and said, "I will give you whatever you wish for saving my daughter. Please tell me what you desire."

But since kindness was his pleasure and happiness itself was his reward, Hoderi expected nothing for his good deed. "It is enough that I was given the honour of rescuing your daughter," Hoderi said humbly.

Gravely the dragon king shook his head. "No, you must have a reward."

Hoderi glanced around the hall. "Very well," he said. "I should like to have that." He pointed to the farthest wall, where a milky-white shell shimmered in the distance. A sudden hush fell over the hall. All eyes turned to Hoderi.

"That," said the great dragon king, "is the magic ear. There is not another one like it in all of Neriya."

"Then you must keep it," Hoderi said quickly. "I have no need of a reward."

The dragon king was silent for a long time. Finally he spoke. "You have saved my daughter's life," he said. "Nothing is too good for you. You must take the magic ear." The king nodded, and one of his subjects removed the magic ear from its special place and handed it with great ceremony to Hoderi.

Tucking the ear safely under his arm, Hoderi climbed on top of the carp for the journey back to the surface. When they landed on the beach, the messenger spoke again.

"The magic ear can bring you great happiness," she told him. "It will let you understand all the earth's creatures. But you must keep it well hidden from those who wish to use it only for their own means."

As Hoderi hurried along the beach and up the path to the nobleman's house, he could hear the sparrows singing their midday song, *chuu, chuu, chuu.* He decided to try the magic ear. Lifting it gently to his own ear, he heard, "Human beings think they are smart, but they know nothing. The stepping stone at the foot of this very tree is solid gold, and no one has discovered it."

oderi walked forward to the tree where the sparrows were perched. There, covered with moss, was the stepping stone the birds spoke about. Hoderi picked it up and rubbed it back and forth on his cotton trousers. It was a solid lump of glittering gold.

Hoderi hid both the gold and magic ear underneath his jacket and continued his walk to the nobleman's gate. There a sign caught his eye. It said, "If anyone can heal my daughter, he shall be given whatever he desires as a reward."

Now, Hoderi knew of the nobleman's daughter. He had seen her move through the garden in her multicoloured robes. She was a smiling young girl who loved to linger near the tea ceremony pavilion in the shade of a red maple. She would toss the birds and other creatures crumbs from her rice-flour cakes. In his heart Hoderi called her the rainbow princess.

A nd now the rainbow princess was ill. For the first time in his life, Hoderi felt great sadness. Determined to help, he walked to the nobleman's back door. After stating his purpose, he was ushered inside.

"I am here to help," he said, bowing low before the nobleman. Great bursts of laughter greeted Hoderi's pronouncement. The nobleman himself was silent, but at his side were his trusted doctors.

"If we are unable to cure the young woman, then surely this dirty, ragged peasant cannot help," the doctors jeered.

But the nobleman loved his daughter and wanted her well so she could wander through the garden once more. "Go to her room," he commanded Hoderi, "and tell me what is wrong."

Hoderi followed an old woman to the room of the rainbow princess. Silently she lay in bed. Her eyes were closed. Her face was drawn. She was scarcely breathing.

Hoderi felt in the folds of his jacket for the magic ear. Surely it should help him now, when the nobleman's daughter was so ill. Lifting it to his ear, Hoderi listened. But he heard nothing. There were no foxes, no birds, not even a mosquito to tell him what was wrong with the rainbow princess who fed them crumbs from her rice-flour cakes.

Saddened, Hoderi went back to the nobleman. "I do not know what is wrong," he said in his true and honest way. "But I will return when I do."

The jeering laughter of the doctors followed Hoderi as he walked out to the garden to begin his work. It was strangely silent that afternoon. There was no cluster of birds in the red maple; even the giant salamander that lived in the bamboo grove was not in his usual place.

oderi toiled long into the night, hoping the salamander might return or that a small frog would journey to the pond near the tea ceremony pavilion. But no one came. Finally, when the stars were out and Hoderi was ready to return to his small hut, he heard the hoot of an owl.

He reached under the folds of his coat for the magic ear and heard the words, "All the doctors and medicines in the world will not cure the nobleman's daughter. For when the roof of her father's house was being thatched, a snake was caught in with the thatching grass. The snake must be freed and fed if the girl is to recover."

Hoderi quickly concealed the magic ear in the folds of his coat and hurried back to the nobleman's house. "I know what is wrong," he told the nobleman. "The disease is a curse, brought on by a snake buried in the roof thatching. You must remove the snake and feed it."

The doctors laughed and jeered even louder than before.

ut the nobleman loved his daughter and wanted her well so she could wander through the garden once more. "Call the thatchers," he said, "and have them tear off the roof thatching."

So it was that the thatchers were pulled from their homes and rushed to the house of the nobleman. Quickly they went to work digging up the thatching. Soon they found the snake, nearly dead from hunger and in great agony.

The nobleman rushed to give it some rice. It ate a little and crawled a little. As it did, the rainbow princess sat up.

"Give it more rice," Hoderi called. The snake was given more rice, and it crawled a little farther. The rainbow princess smiled and stood up.

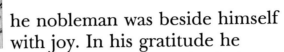he nobleman was beside himself with joy. In his gratitude he bowed low before Hoderi. "You have healed my daughter," he said. "You may have anything you wish as a reward."

But for Hoderi, kindness was his pleasure and happiness was his reward. "There is nothing I desire," he told the nobleman. For once in his life, however, Hoderi was not being honest. There was one thing the young peasant yearned for more than anything in the world. He desired the rainbow princess for his wife.

"Please," the nobleman pleaded. "There must be something you wish for."

Hoderi looked again at the rainbow princess. She was so beautiful. So kind. "Yes," he finally admitted. "I would like to marry your daughter."

The doctors laughed. "You cannot allow this dirty, ragged peasant to marry your daughter," they told the nobleman.

Now, the nobleman was honest. He had agreed to give Hoderi anything he desired. But the nobleman was also wise. He knew if he angered his subjects, they could give him much grief. He thought for a long time before he answered.

ery well," the nobleman told Hoderi. "I will give you my daughter on one condition: that you have enough wealth to care for her all of her days."

The doctors smirked and giggled and rocked back on their heels. This dirty ragged peasant had not the means to care for the nobleman's daughter. Anyone could see that.

But Hoderi reached under the folds of his coat and pulled out the solid lump of gold. "I believe this will take care of your daughter and our children for all of their days."

The doctors stopped smirking and giggling and stared at the gold in disbelief. But the nobleman smiled. "I believe it will," he said with a nod.

From that day forward Hoderi and his rainbow princess lived in perfect splendour with the nobleman and his household. Every morning at dawn Hoderi and his wife would go to the pavilion with their pockets full of rice-cake crumbs. And before anyone was awake to watch them, they would take turns listening to all the creatures in the garden with the dragon king's magic ear.

To the magic in my life, Zachary and Tlell
L.L.

To my friend and partner Barbara Weaver-Bosson
whose love and support is without bounds.

I would also like to dedicate this work to Margaret and
Alfred Bosson without whom, as Mr. and Mrs. Professor
Floydd Mackenzie so aptly stated, none of this would
have happened.
V.B.

Text copyright © 1995 Laura Langston
Illustration copyright © 1995 Victor Bosson

Canadian Cataloguing in Publication Data
Langston, Laura, 1958–
The magic ear

ISBN 1-55143-035-5 (bound)
I. Bosson, Victor, 1946– II. Title.
PS8573.A5832M33 1995   jC813'.54   C95-910449-6   PZ7.L36Ma 1995

Publication assistance provided by The Canada Council.

Design by Victor Bosson
Printed and bound in Hong Kong

Orca Book Publishers Ltd.
P.O. Box 5626, Station B
Victoria, BC Canada
V8R 6S4

Orca Book Publishers Ltd.
P.O. Box 468
Custer, WA USA
98240-0468

10 9 8 7 6 5 4 3 2 1